I AM ENOUGH

A Groundbreaking Self-Awareness Guide For Women

LaTersa Blakely

Also by LaTersa Blakely:

Momproneur~Steps to balance work, life & love

From Brokenness To Greatness~A Guide to living beyond your past & stepping into your Greatness

I AM ENOUGH!

A Groundbreaking Self Awareness Guide For Women

LaTersa Blakely

Published by LaTersa Blakely Enterprises, Inc.

ISBN-13:9780615966250

ISBN-10: 061596625X

LaTersa Blakely Enterprises, Inc.
Website: www.latersablakely.com
Facebook: www.facebook.com/authorlatersablakely
Twitter: www.twitter.com/latersablakely
Blog: www.momswearingmultiplehats.com

Acknowledgements

This book is dedicated to my little princess, Sarah Lynise Blakely. I really am so blessed to have such an amazing daughter like you. I remember way before I ever had kids or even when I was about your age, I used to play with my baby dolls and tell my mother that one day, I wanted to have a little girl so I could have someone to play dress up with because I didn't have a biological sister; I was blessed with only brothers. I used to play with every little baby girl that came my way because I just thought they were so cute. People in my neighborhood knew how much I loved playing with baby dolls, so they would all save their baby diapers and clothes for me so I could put them on my dolls. Well, God granted me my wish when I found out the sex of my second child, which is you, my little princess. The nurse said, "Ms. Hampton (my maiden name), you are having a girl." I thought she was playing with me, but then I looked at the sonogram, and sure enough, nothing was jiggling in the middle so that day is when it was official that I was having my baby girl. I named you Sarah because in the Bible, it means princess, and that's truly what you are. If I am ever out of reach, on your journey to becoming an adult and you doubt my love for you, I want you to read this book and know that I want nothing but the best for you. Mommy loves you more than words could ever say. And know that you are Special and Amazing!

A BLOSSOMING WOMAN'S PROMISE

I promise to love me unconditionally no matter what.

I promise to value my body.

I am God's favorite daughter.

I promise to only use my words to speak greatness about myself.

I am all that and a bag of chips!

I promise to do my best to take good care of me.

I am Fabulous!

I promise to seek guidance when I need to.

I am an goal achiever!

I promise to learn from my mistakes.

I deserve the absolute best!

I am wonderfully and fearfully made!

You Sow To Grow!

Never Plant Bad Thoughts In Your Mental Garden!

AM

I

ENOUGH

Dear Blossoming Woman:

You sow to grow so that you can blossom into that beautiful woman God created you to be. You have to know that you are enough and that everything you need is already on the inside of you. When you look in the mirror, you should see a beautiful reflection of you and a smile coming right back at you. Just know that as you get older and wiser, your body will begin to change, and it is nothing for you to get alarmed about; it's just a sign that you are maturing and sprouting into a beautiful seasoned woman.

Always know that if you get to a point in your life where you don't like something, remember this little prayer that my mother and auntie used to say to me. It's called The Serenity Prayer:

"God, grant me the serenity
to accept the things I cannot change;
courage to change the things I can;
and wisdom to know the difference."

It wasn't until I was older that I truly understood what it meant, but I want to take a moment to explain it to you. This prayer is simply telling you that if you can change something about you that you are not pleased with, know that it's within your power to do so. For instance, if you think you are too fat, you can exercise daily, and change your eating habits.

Also, it tells you to accept the things that you cannot change. This means that you might have had some bad things to happen to you, but that is something you cannot change, so you have to find it within your soul to accept it and move forward with your life. The last portion says "to grant you the wisdom to know the difference"; this means you have to be able to distinguish the difference between things you can change and things you cannot change. Repeat this prayer over and over again until you memorize it.

You can never get away from yourself, and you will always be with you so you have to learn how to love yourself through the good and the bad times. Know that God love you very much and adore you.

Remember, it is up to you to make your dreams happen! It's not your parents' responsibility, your friends', nor your church family's to do it for you. You have to water and nurture your dreams on a daily basis because faith without works is dead. I wonder what dreams are lying dormant in your heart; have you given it any thought? My baby girl is five-years-old, and she tells me every day that she wants to be a makeup artist because she feels every girl and woman should be beautiful. She also says she wants to be a ballerina because she loves to dance. Now, the funny thing is she wants to be five different things, but you know what I say to her? "Sarah, baby girl, you can be anything you want to be as long as you give it your all and work hard towards making your dreams a reality."

One last thing, no matter what the world says or your friends, family members or anybody says you are, you are beautiful, wonderfully and fearfully made. When God created you, he created something unique and special that only you can fulfill in this lifetime. Don't let anyone make you feel like you are not worthy or that your life doesn't matter because it does. Because you were born, this world is now a better place since your beautiful, blossoming self is alive and well.

Enjoy your life and make great memories because this world is such a beautiful place, and it has some amazing things to offer you. Be respectful and kind to others and always wear a smile on your face. My grandmother used to tell me, "Gal, if you frown then the world will frown right along with you; but also if you smile, the world will smile right back at you." So, wear your smile with pride and dignity. Always do your best, give 110 percent at all times, and never be afraid to make mistakes. Know that failure is a part of life, and in those valuable lessons you will learn things to get you one step closer to your destiny.

I love you beautiful blossoming woman, and my prayer and hope for you is to continue to sow so that you can blossom and GROW!

LaTersa Blakely,

CEO/Founder

LaTersa Blakely Enterprises, Inc.

Let's Get To The Root of It

My mind is my Garden

I am planting seeds of loving thoughts of me!

My Body Is My Tree!

I believe I am Special

I know I am Beautiful

I nourish and love my body every day!

My emotions and feelings are all mine

I choose to feel great about myself

I feel good when I look in the mirror and see a reflection of me

I feel powerful because I know I am worth every amazing thing that comes my
way

What Types Of Seeds You Are Growing in Your Mental Garden?

It takes 21 days to form a new habit, so for the next 21 days, I want you to make a new declaration over your life by sowing new seeds. Don't get scared, I'm not talking about going to the field and chopping cotton (I chopped cotton from the ages of 12 to 16). I want you to dig up the old negative beliefs about yourself and start fresh with blossoming seeds so that by the end of your 21 days, you will be sprouting all over the place.

I SOW TO GROW

28 DAYS OF AFFIRMATIONS FOR Women

Day One

Affirmation: I sow seeds of love for myself because God made me fearfully and wonderfully. I will only focus on what is right with me and not what is wrong with me. God's love for me is never ending and is unconditional.

Seed Action Tip: Write down five things you love about yourself. Post them on sticky notes, and place them throughout your room (make sure you ask your parent's permission first).

_____

_____

_____

_____

_____

_____

_____

_____

_____

_____

_____

_____

_____

_____

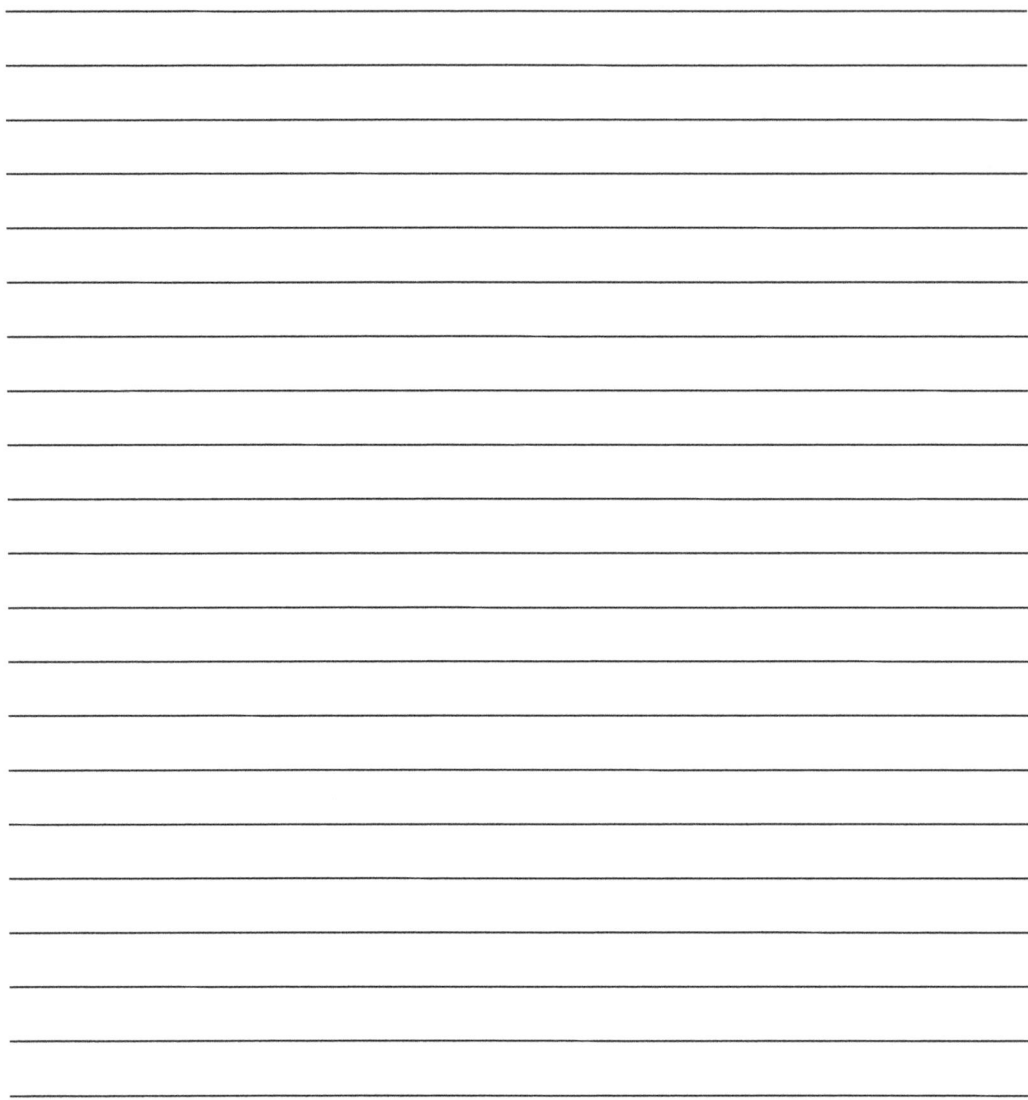

Day Two

Affirmation of the day: I sow seeds of approval. I am approved by myself and God. I don't need approval from other people or outside resources to feel good about myself. I can see the wonderful qualities God has blessed me with.

Seed Tip Action: Repeat this throughout your day five to 10 times: "I am approved by myself and God."

_____

_____

_____

_____

_____

_____

_____

_____

_____

_____

_____

_____

_____

_____

_____

_____

_____

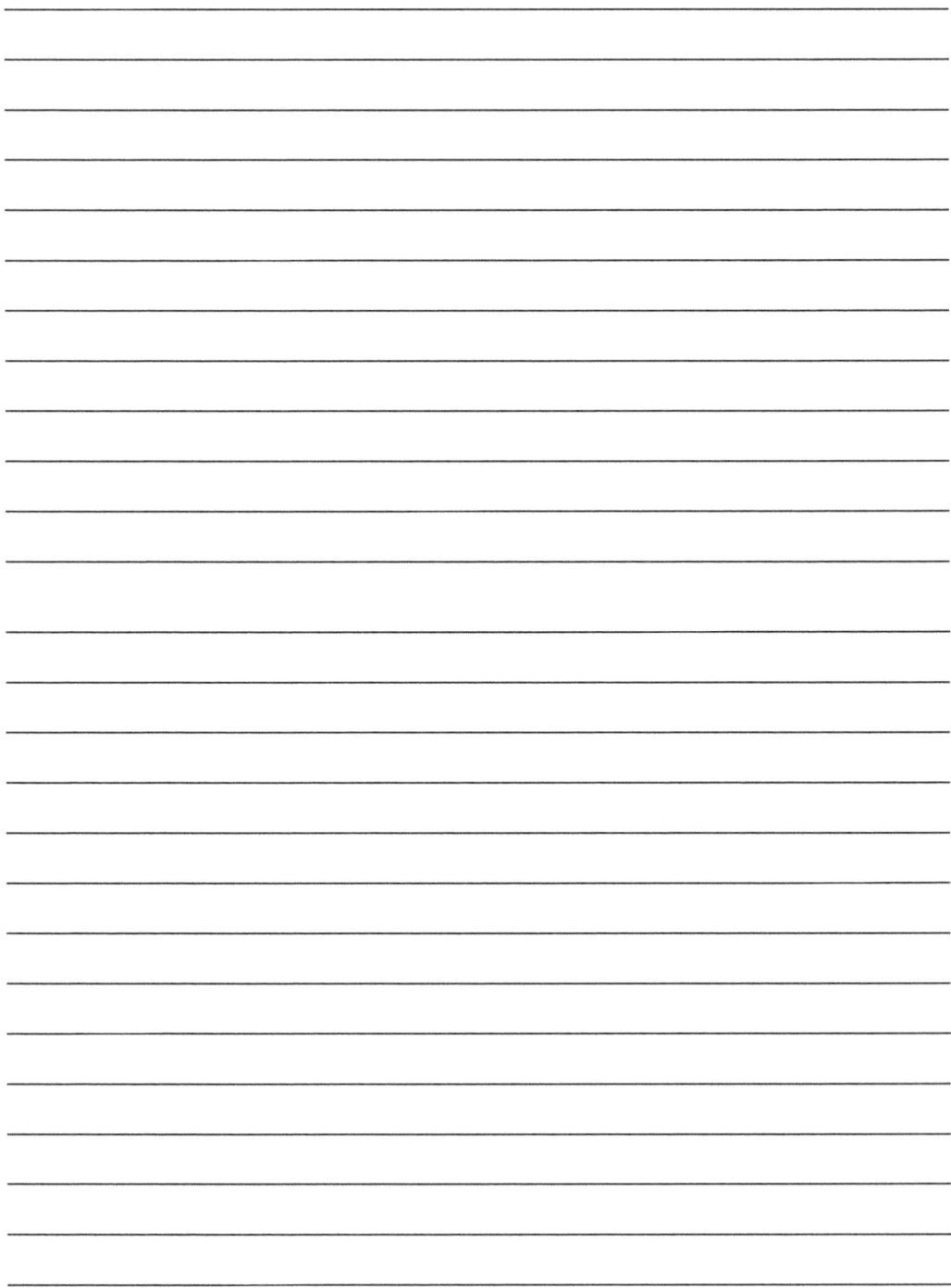

Day Three

Affirmation of the day: I sow seeds of beauty. I am beautiful and fabulous in every way. I can take and appreciate compliments from others. I know that real beauty comes from within, and it's not about wearing makeup.

Seed Action Tip: Repeat this, and write it on your note book and mirrors: "I am Beautiful."_____

_____

_____

_____

_____

_____

_____

_____

_____

_____

_____

_____

_____

_____

_____

_____

_____

_____

Day Four

Affirmation of the day: I sow seeds of gratefulness. I am grateful for the life I've been given, and I will show my appreciation to God by not complaining.

Seed Tip Action: Write down 10 things you are grateful for throughout the day.

_____

_____

_____

_____

_____

_____

_____

_____

_____

_____

_____

_____

_____

_____

_____

_____

_____

_____

_____

Day Five

Affirmation of the day: I sow seeds of having a positive attitude. I will only think and speak on things that are healthy and positive about myself.

Seed Action Tip: Read and memorize this bible verse: Phillipians 4:8, "Finally, brothers and sisters, whatever is true,, whatever is noble, what so ever is right, what so ever is pure, whatever is lovely, whatever is admirable, if anything is excellent or praiseworthy ~ think on these things.

_____

_____

_____

_____

_____

_____

_____

_____

_____

_____

_____

_____

_____

_____

Day Six

Affirmation of the day: I sow seeds of purity. I will keep my body clean and smelling good at all times. I will cherish and respect it by saving myself until I'm married. I will not partake in any harmful or unhealthy activities that will cause harm or damage to my body.

Seed Action Tip: I will respect myself and my body at all times. Write down five ways you will do this daily

_____

_____

_____

_____

_____

_____

_____

_____

_____

_____

_____

_____

_____

_____

_____

_____

Day Seven

Affirmation of the day: I sow seeds of goals. I will set goals for myself and dream big. I will work hard and do my best to make things happen. I promise to keep God first at all times in my life.

Seed Action Tip: I will create a plan to achieve my goals, and I will work my plan and do something every day to manifest my dreams. Use the next few pages to do so.

_____

_____

_____

_____

_____

_____

_____

_____

_____

_____

_____

_____

_____

_____

_____

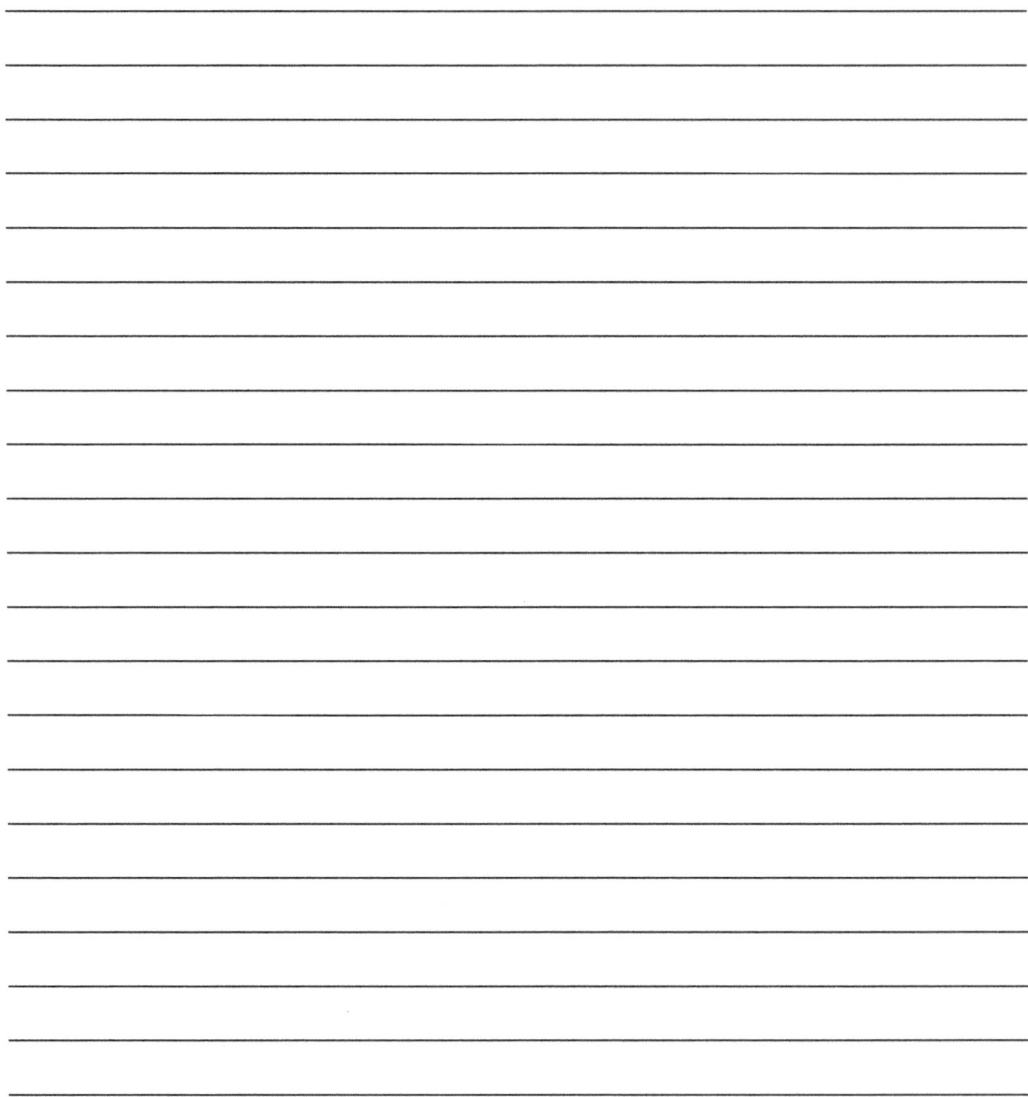

Day Eight

Affirmation of the day: I sow seeds of God's unconditionally love for me. I am a one-of-a-kind blossoming woman.

Seed Action Tip: Find three Bible verses that speak about how much God loves you.

_____

_____

_____

_____

_____

_____

_____

_____

_____

_____

_____

_____

_____

_____

_____

_____

_____

_____

Day Nine

Affirmation of the day: I sow seeds of encouragement. I only use my words to lift me up, not tear me down. I only speak positive words over my life.

Seed Action Tip: Repeat five positive adjectives that describe yourself (examples: beautiful, loving, etc.).

_____

_____

_____

_____

_____

_____

_____

_____

_____

_____

_____

_____

_____

_____

_____

_____

_____

Day Ten

Affirmation of the day: I sow seeds of Self-Approval. I will not seek approval of others because God and I approve myself.

Seed Action Tip: I will hug myself and love on me daily. I will write down the first five thoughts that come to mind when I think of myself.

_____

_____

_____

_____

_____

_____

_____

_____

_____

_____

_____

_____

_____

_____

_____

_____

Day Eleven

Affirmation of the day: I sow seeds of respect. I will respect myself and others at all times. I will not be disrespectful.

Seed Action Tip: For the next 24 hours, I want you to be conscious of how you treat yourself and how you treat others. Keep notes in your journal and record your actions throughout today.

_____

_____

_____

_____

_____

_____

_____

_____

_____

_____

_____

_____

_____

_____

_____

_____

_____

Day Twelve

Affirmation of the day: I sow seeds of excellence. Everything that I attempt to do will be done with integrity and excellence.

Seed Action Tip: From this point on — no matter if it's washing dishes — you must do it with excellence. Record your progress in your journal today.

_____

_____

_____

_____

_____

_____

_____

_____

_____

_____

_____

_____

_____

_____

_____

_____

_____

Day Thirteen

Affirmation of the day: I sow seeds of Power.

Seed Action Tip: Repeat the following words 10 times a day: "I am Powerful beyond measure." Write them down in your journal today as well.

_____

_____

_____

_____

_____

_____

_____

_____

_____

_____

_____

_____

_____

_____

_____

_____

_____

_____

Day Fourteen

Affirmation of the day: I sow seeds of great talents. I am gifted with amazing talents and gifts, and I will use them to serve and bless others.

Seed Action Tip: Write down all the things you are good at. Now, commit to using your gifts each and every day. (Remember, if you don't use your gifts/talents, you can definitely lose them)._____

_____

_____

_____

_____

_____

_____

_____

_____

_____

_____

_____

_____

_____

_____

_____

_____

Day Fifteen

Affirmation of the day: I sow seeds of acceptance. I choose to accept myself just the way God made me.

Seed Action Tip: I will build upon my strengths and not focus so much on my weaknesses. I will use my strengths to do amazing and great things today.

_____

_____

_____

_____

_____

_____

_____

_____

_____

_____

_____

_____

_____

_____

_____

_____

_____

_____

_____

_____

_____

Day Sixteen

Affirmation of the day. I sow seeds of love for my body. I love my hips, thighs, hair, face, nose and every other body part that God has blessed me with.

Seed Action Tip: I will take proper care of my body by nourishing it with love, soap and water on a daily basis. Fill in the blank, and repeat: I love my body because_____.

Things I can do to better love my body today are:

_____

_____

_____

_____

_____

_____

_____

_____

_____

_____

_____

_____

_____

_____

_____

_____

Day Seventeen

Affirmation of the day: I sow seeds of faith.

Seed Action Tip: Repeat these words: "I will use my faith and hope to overcome life's challenges." Memorize the Bbible verse: Faith Without Works Is Dead today.

_____

_____

_____

_____

_____

_____

_____

_____

_____

_____

_____

_____

_____

_____

_____

_____

_____

_____

_____

_____

Day Eighteen

Affirmation of the day: I sow seeds of believing. I will believe and see the good in myself and others.

Seed Action Tip: Repeat five times per day: "I believe I can BE, DO & HAVE anything that my heart so desires."_____

_____

_____

_____

_____

_____

_____

_____

_____

_____

_____

_____

_____

_____

_____

_____

_____

_____

Day Nineteen

Affirmation of the day: I sow seeds of forgiveness. I will choose to practice the act of forgiveness on a daily basis.

Seed Action Tip: Write a letter to each individual that you need to forgive. Place it in an envelope, and throw it in the trash. This is your way of releasing the negative energy that sticks with you when you don't practice forgiveness.

_____

_____

_____

_____

_____

_____

_____

_____

_____

_____

_____

_____

_____

_____

_____

_____

_____

Day Twenty

Affirmation of the day: I sow seeds of kindness.

Seed Action Tip: I will be kind to myself and every person that encounters my space (including your spouse/children/co-workers, too).

_____

_____

_____

_____

_____

_____

_____

_____

_____

_____

_____

_____

_____

_____

_____

_____

_____

_____

_____

_____

Day Twenty-One

Affirmation of the day: I sow seeds of prayer. I will seek God in everything that I do by praying on a daily basis.

Seed Action Tip: Learn the Lord's Prayer, and write it down five times (also, ask your parents to help you with learning this prayer.)_____

_____

_____

_____

_____

_____

_____

_____

_____

_____

_____

_____

_____

_____

_____

_____

_____

_____

_____

Hey you, yes you!

So how does it feel now that you've planted some new seeds in your mental garden? By now, you should be experiencing some feelings of joy on the inside. I pray that you have been doing the assignments on a daily basis; if not go back, refresh, and do this as many times as you need to.

There is no rush; you can go about this at your own pace.

I love you girlies,

Sow in Love,

LaTersa

A girl is never too old to treat herself to her favorite comfy cozies

There will be some days that you are not feeling so positive or will not be in such a great mood, so I want to share with you a few things that every blossoming woman must carry in her tool bag. I still love my teddy bears (must be fluffy), and I still write in my journals daily. I've found that writing in my journal helps me see things for what they really are.

The following items are some of my favorite things and some of the things I used when I was a little girl. If you don't have all of the things below, just use what you have until you can purchase the rest of them.

1.   A pink pen

2.   A pink journal or notebook

3.   A fluffy pink teddy bear

4.   A bottle of all-natural bubble baths (vanilla, strawberry or your favorite scent)

5.   A package of sugar-free gum

6.   A bag of your favorite fruits (grapes, strawberries, apples, etc.; it keeps you from eating candy.)

7.   Faith. You will need faith to manifest your dreams.

8.   A pink and green lingerie set

9.   White cotton sheets for your bed

10.   A beautiful blossoming tree (a place where you can go and write in your journal)

11.   A package of Kleenex® Cottonelle®

12.   A bottle of your favorite nail polish (pink, green, white, etc.)

13.   A cute calendar (to keep note of all of your fun-in-the-sun days)

14.   A sacred space to pray (My favorite place to pray is in my bed; I pray before I even step a foot out of the bed.)

15.   A Great Inspirational Book or two

A Blossoming Woman's Survival Solutions

On those days when you are sad and feel like you've lost your best friend, the following will help cheer you up:

1.   Take a soothing bath using your favorite bubble baths/oils.

2.   Put on your cute, pink lingerie set.

3.   Write in your pink journal (journaling is therapeutic for your soul).

On those days when you feel angry, try these:

1.   Go to your sacred space and pray.

2.   Eat some of those delicious fruits.

3.   Write in your pink journal.

When you are feeling like you're all alone, try these:

1.   Write how you feel in your journal.

2.   Read it out loud.

3.   Give yourself a big, blossoming hug.

WHAT'S SPROUTING IN YOUR MIND

In the next few pages, I want you to write down what's on your mind. How are you feeling about yourself at this very moment?

I want my heart to feel good and my outer appearance to look good.

_____

_____

_____

_____

_____

_____

My heart will feel better when I

_____

_____

_____

_____

_____

_____

_____

Two things I can do today to feel better are

_____

_____

_____

_____

_____

_____

I feel happy when I

_____

_____

_____

_____

_____

When I am happy, I feel

_____

_____

_____

_____

_____

_____

_____

I feel sad when I

_____

_____

_____

_____

_____

_____

When I am sad, I feel like

_____

_____

_____

_____

_____

_____

_____

_____

_____

I love my body because

_____
_____
_____
_____
_____
_____
_____

Three things I love about my body are

_____
_____
_____
_____
_____
_____
_____

What I don't like about my body

_____

_____

_____

_____

_____

_____

_____

What can I do to love my body more?

_____

_____

_____

_____

_____

_____

_____

My life is not going the way I want because

_____

_____

_____

_____

_____

_____

_____

My life will be great when I

_____

_____

_____

_____

_____

_____

_____

_____

LET'S BE HONEST

I really want

_____

_____

_____

_____

_____

_____

_____

If I receive what I want, I will feel

_____

_____

_____

_____

_____

_____

_____

The things I hate doing are

_____

_____

_____

_____

_____

I hate doing these things because

_____

_____

_____

_____

_____

_____

If I died today, what do I want everyone to know about me?

_____

_____

_____

_____

_____

_____

_____

_____

If I died today, I think people will say this about me

_____

_____

_____

_____

_____

_____

_____

If I could start my life over again, I would want this to be different

_____

_____

_____

_____

_____

_____

_____

_____

If things were to change, I believe I would be

_____

_____

_____

_____

_____

_____

_____

_____

_____

Anything is Possible When You Believe

What I truly want to accomplish is

_____

_____

_____

_____

_____

_____

Write down your dream statement. Les Brown, a speaker and author, has a quote that says: "Shoot for the moon, even if you don't reach it, at least you will be among the stars.

Write the vision, and make it plain.

I dream about becoming

_____

_____

_____

_____

_____

_____

Now, create your Plant Your Vision Dream Book. You can grab another one of your pretty pink journals, and use it for this fun project. (Items you'll need include scissors, glue sticks, a hole puncher and markers or crayons.)

1.   Get tons of magazines.

2.   Cut out pictures, and create your dream with words and beautiful photos.

3.   Include a picture of you.

4.   Use glue sticks to paste your images in your book.

Remember, you can BE, DO and HAVE anything your pretty little heart so desires because you are wonderfully and fearfully made and you are ENOUGH.

More Affirmations:

1.   I Dream a Garden Full of Love for Me!

2.   I Dream a Garden Full of Hope for Me!

3.   I Dream a Life that is Fierce!

YOU ARE THE BOMB.COM!

YOU ARE ENOUGH!!!

When I take care of myself,

When I am honoring my body and soul,

When I am honest with myself,

I BLOSSOM lovely!

I am FABULOUS!

The following is a checklist of things you should remember and know about yourself.

Complete this list today, and refer back to it every three months

My favorite food is

_____

_____

_____

This is my favorite food because

_____

_____

_____

My favorite color is

_____

_____

_____

This is my favorite color because

_____

_____

_____

My favorite song is

_____

_____

_____

This is my favorite song because

_____

_____

_____

My greatest strength is

_____

_____

_____

My weakness is

_____

_____

_____

I believe I can make my weakness a strength by

_____

_____

_____

My best talent/gift is

_____

_____

_____

I need the most mentoring in

_____

_____

_____

_____

My biggest mistake has been

_____

_____

_____

_____

_____

_____

What I've learned from my mistakes is

_____

_____

_____

_____

_____

_____

I am fearful of this because

_____

_____

_____

_____

_____

Your Mind Is A Garden &

Your Thoughts are Your Seeds

The life I see is a reflection of my seed thoughts.

What thoughts are you thinking?

If you focus your attention and energy on the harvest you desire, that is exactly what will manifest right before your eyes! So be mindful of what you give your time and energy to. Time is your most valuable asset, and once it's gone, you can never get it back.

I want my life to be

_____

_____

_____

_____

_____

_____

_____

_____

I wish my life was

_____

_____

_____

_____

_____

_____

_____

I think my life should be

_____

_____

_____

_____

_____

_____

_____

_____

If your life is not going the way you planned go back and check the kinds of seeds you have planted.

Always focus on what you desire and not what you don't want!

Seed Reflections from your soul

_____

_____

_____

_____

_____

_____

_____

_____

_____

_____

_____

_____

_____

_____

_____

_____

_____

_____

_____

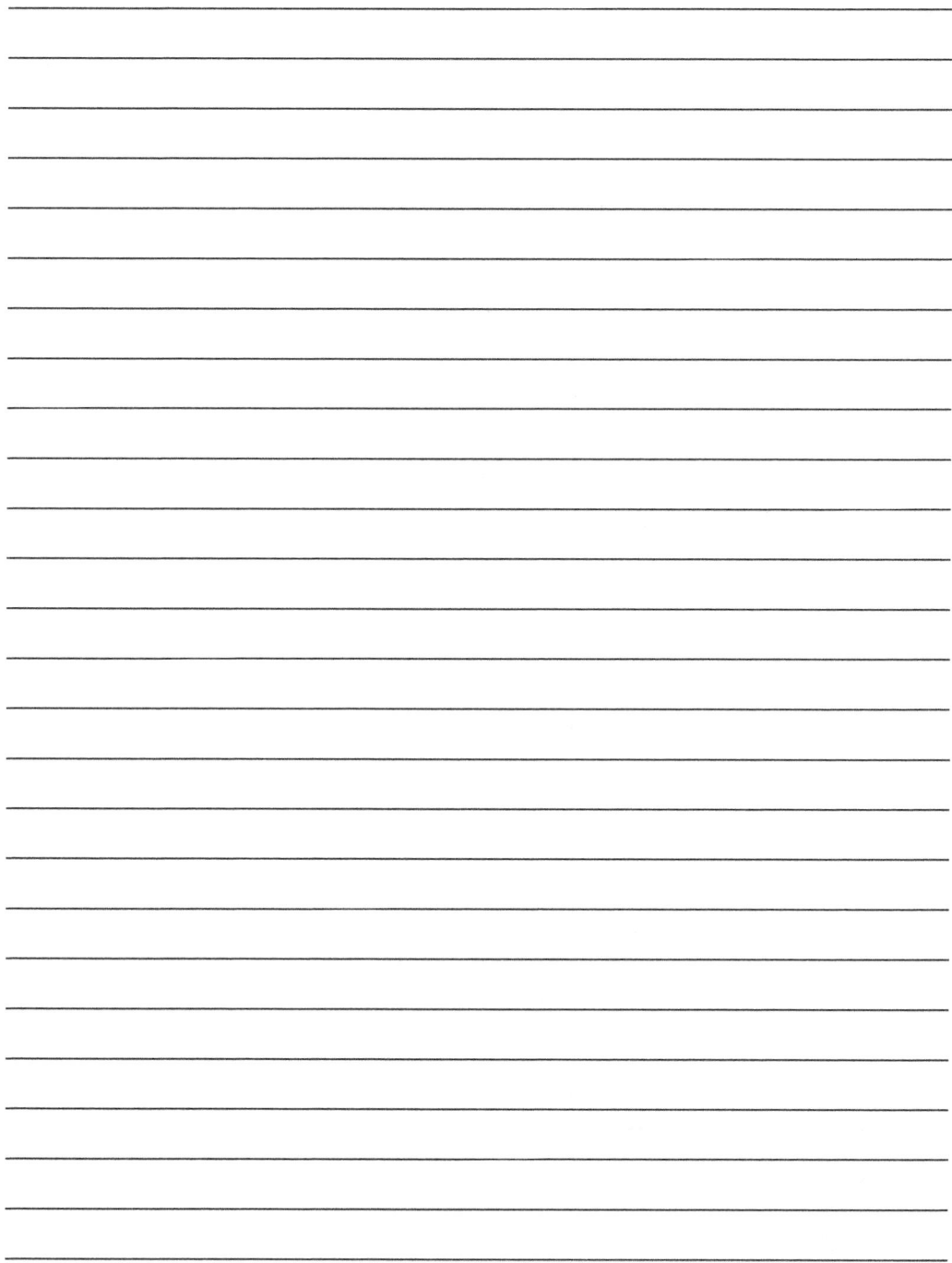

_____

_____

_____

_____

_____

_____

_____

A list of activities to engage in daily

- Exercise (jump rope, jog, dance, etc.).

- Drink plenty of water.

- Laugh a lot.

- Pray, Pray, Pray (My 3Ps).

- Communicate with your spouse/boyfriend.

- Communicate with your children.

- Write in your pink journal.

- Love on someone daily.

- Take care of your personal hygiene daily (a blossoming woman always showers twice per day, brushes her teeth twice per day, etc.).

- Smile at all times (remember, if you smile, the world smiles right back at you).

- Be honest.

- Never be afraid to be different.

- Always value and respect yourself and your body.

- Be kind to others.

- Obey the word (bible).

- Love yourself and hug you daily.

- Never participate in an activity that doesn't feel right to you.

- Always trust your gut.

- Try not to gossip (I know it can be tempting).

- Never repeat anything about yourself that you don't want the world to know.

- Be sociable (join meetup groups, attend family gatherings, join associations or organizations, etc.) .

- Never stop learning (keep an open mind to learn new things).

- Eat a variety of healthy foods, snacks and drinks daily (fruits, nuts, naked juices, water, baked foods, belVita breakfast cookies, peanut butter crackers, etc.).

- Read a book daily (something empowering, motivational, or inspirational).

- Dedicate your time to learning something new every month (for example, learn how to speak a new language, learn how to cook a new dish, learn a skill that will allow you to get paid for it)

Great books to read:

- ❖ Mompreneur~Steps to balance work, life and love by LaTersa Blakely

- ❖ First Steps To Wealth by Dani Johnson

- ❖ Stillettos in the Kitchen by Shanel Cooper-Sykes

- ❖ How to Let Go & Let God by Regina Baker

- ❖ Declarations of A kingdom Driven Entrepreneur by Candace Ford

- ❖ Sunday Mourning by Rhachelle Nicol

- ❖ The Day She Left by Tamara Gooch

- ❖ The Road To Redemption by Lucinda Cross

- ❖ Happy Women Live Better by Valorie Burton

- ❖ The Confident Woman by Joyce Meyers

- ❖ "Believe in yourself! Have faith in your abilities! Without a humble but reasonable confidence in your own powers you cannot be successful or happy." ~Norman Vincent Peale

- ❖ "If you don't design your own life plan, chances are you'll fall into someone else's plan. And guess what they have planned for you? Not much." ~**Jim Rohn**

- ❖ "Happiness does not depend on what happens to us, but on how we react to what happens to us." ~ Dada JP Vaswani

- ❖ "Surround yourself with only people who are going to lift you higher." ~**Oprah Winfrey**

- ❖ "Do the one thing you think you cannot do. Fail at it. Try again. Do better the second time. The only people who never tumble are those who never mount the high wire. This is your moment. Own it." ~**Oprah Winfrey**

- ❖ "Your thoughts become your words and your attitude. Where the mind goes, man will follow" ~**Joyce Meyers**

- ❖ "You are wonderfully and fearfully made" ~**Almighty God**

- ❖ "On your way to discovering yourself, don't forget to reach back and sow a seed of love into the next young girl's life." ~**LaTersa Blakely**

❖ "Always continue the climb. It is possible for you to do whatever you choose, if you first get to know who you are and are willing to work with a power that is greater than ourselves to do it." ~Ella Wheeler Wilcox

❖ "Always do your best. What you plant now, you will harvest later." ~Og Mandino

❖ "Act as if what you do makes a difference. It does." ~William James

Dear Blossoming Woman,

My prayer is for you to blossom into that beautiful woman God has created you to become. I hope you will implement the assignments and start to plant seeds of excellence, joy, love, patience, kindness, success and all those great things I know you already have within you. I want to hear from you and see how you are doing. I'm always here for you, so feel free to join me on Facebook at our Finding Your Joy fan page: http://www.facebook.com/authorlatersablakely

I want you to sow so you can continue to BLOSSOM!

You Are Enough,

LaTersa,

CEO/Founder

www.ingramcontent.com/pod-product-compliance
Lightning Source LLC
Chambersburg PA
CBHW031224090426
42740CB00007B/702